There's Another Me In Me

Sherman Boone

There's Another Me In Me by *Sherman Boone*
Published by *ThroneRoom Expressions*
ThroneRoom Expressions Publishing Headquarters
33 Old Mill Lane
Southampton, PA 18966

Cover Design by *ThroneRoom Expressions & Addison Graphics*
Editing by *ThroneRoom Expressions*.

For more information please contact:
ThroneRoom Expressions Publishing
throneroomexpressions@gmail.com.
info@charphelpsinternational.com
www.charphelpsinternational.com

Library of Congress Control Number: *2022922351*

Printed in the United States

DEDICATION

To Apostle D.C. Thomas and Pastor Sherman Boone Sr.

I am my Fathers' Son

To my wife Seanna

I love you till death, never part.

CONTENTS

INTRODUCTION

Have you ever felt as if you were living in a parallel universe? It feels almost as if there's a better version of you living in another dimension of reality meanwhile you're stuck living in this one. Sometimes you are inwardly frustrated with your life while watching others live out a life that you know within yourself that you were also created for. It's that your envious of others, it's the fact that you know that you were meant and made for more than what you have resigned to become.

One of my fondest memories growing up is that of my mother and her sisters packing my older cousins and myself into a caravan of cars on a Saturday afternoon and going to the mall. I became so fond of it that as I got older I became the preverbal "mallrat:" I would just go to the mall just for the sake of going. As a result, I became an expert at window shopping. I would see outfits that I would imagine myself wearing. Shoes that I thought would go great with that suit, neckties that would go great with that shirt, and so on and so on, you get my drift.

Now, as harmless as it may seem, being window shopper becomes detrimental when you never buy, because what you imagined in your mind never manifests in your hand. That is the inward conflict that many of us have faced and are facing right as you read this. We have spent our lives window shopping the life, relationships, and careers that we believe that we were meant for only, to this point, never attaining it.

That is what this journey we are about to embark on is all about. Bringing you face to face with the Creator's intent of who you were meant to be and making it into who you are. No more window shopping in life. Now is the time to meet the person buried within you beneath the person that self-doubt and trauma has led you to be. There is someone greater within you. There is someone that is more innovative within you. There is someone stronger within you. There is another you in you. Let's begin.

PART I
IDENTITY

"Who am I?" That's a question that everyone at one time of their lives has found themselves asking while searching within the deep corridors of their conscience. To be truthfully honest, I myself, while penning this chapter found myself contemplating that same question. Many times in life we find ourselves constantly redefining ourselves in order to properly fulfill the various roles that the transitions of life call for us to adapt to. It is very easy to see how in the midst of adapting and re-adjusting to the ever changing tides and currents of life, that we lose sight of who we are.

Some people lose sight of who they are in what they do. This trait is very common among men. Men are naturally occupationally oriented; we define ourselves by our ability to provide and our careers which produce the resources necessary to enable us to do so. Adam's first interaction with God was job related. God was the boss and Adam was the employee of the month. Now although working and providing for oneself or family is one of the basic fundamental instincts of any productive human being, what you do cannot be the foundation of who you are. It is an extension of who you are, but it can never define who you are.

What if you lose your job? Do you cease from existing? What if you (God forbid) experience an accident that hinders your physical ability to live an ideal life, much less earn a living? Do you stop living? This is a perplexing reality that all too often ends with someone committing suicide or becoming entangled in a web of criminal activity that leads to suffocating consequences of long term imprisonment. It is this reality that often times put a strain on what was once solid marriages simply because the spouse was unable to find self-worth outside of having a job.

Then there are the other individuals who lose who they are in *what* they are. Now when I say *what* they are, I'm referring to the roles they play in other people's lives. These individuals often times base the significance on the closeness and depth of their relationships with the people around them. This trait is very common among women. They inherit this trait honestly. Adam's first introduction to the world around him was the occupation of naming the animals while Eve's very construction was for sole purpose of relationship. Women are commonly driven by relationship, primarily from the aspect of intimacy. Men are also fueled by relationship, not as much from the aspect of intimacy as it is from the realm of respect. The downside of defining who you are through the roles you play in the relationships in your life is that people change, children grow up, loved ones pass away and unfortunately (God forbid), marriages end in divorce. As a result of these challenging transitions (if you based your identity off of what you do or solely off what role you play in your relationships, when life hits you (and indeed it will) with its unexpected twist and turns) you will find yourself caught in an identity crisis.

Truth be told, I strongly believe that we never come into the full knowledge of who we are within ourselves. Ecclesiastes 3:11 introduces us to very perplexing reality that states,

> He (God) has made everything beautiful in its time. Also He has placed eternity in their (mankind) hearts, except that no one can find the work that God does from beginning to end.[1]

There's an eternal agenda and plan that we find ourselves constantly evolving into that we, at the end of the day, don't have the capacity to fully understand nor comprehend. This can present a very daunting obstacle in answering the question, *Who Am I?* How can I possibly

---

[1] *Ecclesiastes 3:11 – www.biblegateway.com*

answer that question when the validity of the answer I give today may change by tomorrow? How can I possibly define who I am when my understanding of who I am is flawed at best and incomplete in its finality? Intellectuals over centuries have wrestled with this quandary that's at the core of human existence. Yet it is imperative that we find an anchor that's strong enough to grip hold of an eternal truth that will enable us to weather the impending storms of self-discovery and provide an inner platform on which we build a greater understanding of who we are.

The journey we're about to go on, no matter how long or how brief it maybe, is a journey to discover or affirm the *real* you. I'm not talking about the *you* defined by the temporal security of a career or the success of a promotion. I'm not talking about the *you* defined by relationships, that when abruptly dissolved, cease from living beyond the heartbreak. I'm talking about the *you*, not seen through our human eyes of perception, but through the eternal lenses of God into limitless possibility.

In our journey, although we will refer to many other contemporaries from the Bible, our primary template, if you will, will be the Hebrew patriarch Jacob. It's going to be through our in depth look into the life of Jacob, primarily his transformative experience that changed him into Israel, that we will discover the path we all must follow in order to find the other person God has placed in all of us.

PART II

CREATION VS. BIRTH

One night I was watching *TBN* and the late Bishop Kenneth Moles was on as a guest. During his segment he said something that really fascinated me. He said, *"There's a difference between creation and being born."* Now, to be completely honest I vaguely remember the entirety of what he said, but that comment alone was enough to send this inquisitive mind on a treasure hunt for the truth of such a profound statement. What I discovered changed my life and I believe it will change yours too.

Throughout the Bible there so many scriptures that discuss the reality of our existence in the mind and thoughts of God before the world even began. The Book of Ephesians tells us,

> *Blessed be the God and Father of Lord Jesus*
> *Christ, who hath blessed us with all spiritual*
> *blessings in heavenly places in Christ: according*
> *as He hath chosen us in Him before the*
> *foundation of the world, that we should be holy*
> *and without blame before Him in love.[2]*

Not only does the Bible speak of God thinking of us before the foundation of the world, but it also speaks of Him thinking of us before conception. In Psalm 139:16 it states,

---

[2] *Ephesians 1: 3, 4 (KJV) – www.biblegateway.com*

Your eyes saw my substance, being yet

unformed. And in Your book they were all

written, the days fashioned for me, yet when

there were none of them.³

Now, that's a powerful notion for one to consider.
God has already fashioned our days before we even
materialized in our mother's womb. This implies that the
moment I wrote this portion of the book, and the present
moment of you reading this was meant to happen exactly
when it happen. However, as powerful of a revelation
Psalms 139:16 presents, the scripture in the Bible that
speak on this subject, the one that is the most striking is
Jeremiah 1:5. Let's take a look at the revelation that God
reveals to the reluctant prophet. It states,

Before I formed you in your mother's womb

I knew you; before you were born I

sanctified you; I ordained you to be a

prophet to the nations.⁴

Now when I read this scripture within the context
of Bishop Moles comment, it opened my spiritual
understanding to the divine systematic process of creation.
Creation begins with a thought. Notice that God told

---

³ *Psalm 13:16 – www.biblegateway.com*
⁴ *Jeremiah 1:5 – www.biblegateway.com*

Jeremiah, "I knew you;" he was in the foresight of God's mind before conception. The more telling aspect of the scripture is the revealing of the truth that not only was he known of God, but that God knew him according to a divine agenda. This introduces us to the most definitive element that must be addressed if we're ever going to discover who we are and properly assess the scope of our lives – Purpose.

The quintessential question that is the Siamese twin to *Who Am I*, is *"why am I here?"* you can't answer one without venturing into the other. It's the understanding of purpose that shapes my understanding of who I am, and it's the understanding of who I am and how I was created that brings me into full acceptance of purpose. What we have to understand, my brothers and sisters, is that contrary to the ever growing postmodern ideology that has now become prevalent in our society, we the creatures do not possess the authority to determine our purpose.

We have as much authority in the matter as a car telling its manufacture it's going to be a plane. The manufacture purposely left off wings and aerodynamically framed the car, not for flying, but for driving.
If the reality of a definitive purpose is what introduces you to *who* you are then there's no wonder why a sense of

discontentment has grown in our society at an expediential rate. People who are occupationally driven are constantly (voluntarily or involuntarily) changing their careers. People who are relationally driven are constantly changing relational ties; most people don't even have the same circle of friends they had two years ago, and the divorce rate is at an all-time high. We are constantly evolving in the understanding of purpose – a purpose that isn't authored by us, the creation, but by God, the Creator.

Let's take a look at what the Bible declares as the whole duty or purpose of man in Ecclesiastes 12:13. It reads,

> *Let us hear the conclusion of the whole matter: Fear God, and keep his commandments: for this is the whole duty of man.*[5]

In the case of Jacob, this divine purpose was revealed to his mother, Rebekah, who while pregnant with him and his brother, Esau, was experiencing great pain. Here's what God said concerning what was going on within her womb:

> And the Lord said to her: 'Two nations are in your womb, two peoples

---

[5] *Ecclesiastes 12:13 (KJV) – www.biblegateway.com*

shall be separated from your body; one people shall be stronger than the other, and the older (Esau) shall serve the younger (Jacob).[6]

God revealed to Rebekah, Jacob's destiny and purpose before he was born. Now, from reading this particular scripture someone from our day and time may not understand the significance of *"the older shall serve the younger,"* but in that time it was a culture defying notion that the youngest will be superior to the oldest. In that day it was common practice for the father to leave the blessing and more importantly the birthright (something that we'll discuss in greater length later) to the eldest son, but for God to reveal to Rebekah that the birthright was going to the younger went against the status quo of that day.

What an amazing thought; destined to be a game changer; destined and purposed to defy and alter the traditional order of an entire generation. I would like to take this moment disclose to you this notion, God's purpose for your life is far greater than any agenda or plan that you can ever imagine. His dream for your life is far grander than any dream that you can dream of within yourself. And it's in our submission to His master design that we begin to

---

[6] *Genesis 25:23 NKJV- www.biblegateway.com*

understand who we are. You were created with a divine purpose in mind, and life outside of His purpose is empty and in essence, is a shell of what it really could be.

Before a painter paints a masterpiece, the painter sees the painting in their mind first. Before they lay brush to canvas, the painter has envisioned the finished work of art so that every stroke is calculated and precise, bringing about the magnificence they seen in the canvas of their mind. My friend, before one brushstroke touched the canvas of your life, God, the Master Painter, already had in mind His manifesto of your life and the beauty of His purposeful creation.

The difficulty, as we will discover, is that it's long road to the understanding of *who* we are in the eyes of God's purpose from what we have become is the result of what we're born into. As we continue our journey to uncovering who you are let's open our hearts and our minds as we dig beneath the surface that has been built and find the treasure within.

In order to gain a proper perspective of what we were born into in contrast to who we were created to be, I would like to use the example of the first created man, Adam, and the first man ever born, Cain. Adam being created from the dust by the very divine hands of God

Himself, was symbolic of man at his very pinnacle of existence. When God breathed into his nostrils, He breathed in him everything he needed to have dominion over all that He created. His intellect was such an off shoot from God that he possessed the mental capabilities to name all the animals without any direct assistance from God.

There are some things, by the mere fact of you being created, that God has empowered you to have dominion over. Not only did he have the ability to accurately name the animals, but more importantly, he had direct fellowship with God; so much so, that God's voice walked with them during the cool of the day. What an awesome notion of the voice of God walking with you in the cool of the day. His first cognitive awareness of anyone other than himself was God. He had a clear understanding of who he was because he had a clear view of who God was and still is. Due his initial innocence in nature, he had uninterrupted relationship with God.

All was well with Adam until he made the tragic choice to find inward truth outside of God and as a result he discovered that outside the covering of a relationship with one's Creator, life in itself becomes shameful and naked. What's even more startling is that instead of running to God, Adam tried to hide from God realizing that the fig leaves that he'd sewn together wasn't adequate enough to cover what he had become.

Many people in the world today are continuing to try to hide from God – sewing together *fig leaves* in an effort to hide themselves and the world around them from the reality of their shame and their feeling of inadequacy. And instead of facing the God who created them, they aggressively repress the inward truth of Divine reality and foolishly convinced themselves He doesn't exist. A world without God is a world without hope.

Here in lies the plight of Cain. Unlike his father who was divinely shaped and formed from the dust and intrinsically innocent of sin, Cain was formed and shaped in the womb of his mother and had inherited a sinful nature passed down to him through his father. That was Adam's gift to his son and to all mankind, a core desire to find oneself outside of God.

Let's take a moment right here a begin to take a hard look at our life and let's examine what *gift* our fathers have given us that we find ourselves prone to indulge in that we feel gives us relevance outside of God. If we really take an introspective look at our lives, we will without a doubt, discover many parallels between the life we now live and the lives of those who went on before us (we will discuss this more in depth later).

The distinct difference between Cain and Adam is that unlike Adam, who hid himself in shame after he had sinned, Cain arrogantly presented himself before God and expected God to accept his failure of heart. When he witnessed God accept the sacrifice of his younger brother, he became jealous. Let's take a look at the account as it's told in Genesis 4:3-7. The Bible says:

> *And in the process of time it came to pass, that Cain brought of the fruit of the ground an offering unto the Lord. And Abel, he also brought of the firstlings of his flock and the fat thereof. And the Lord had respect unto Abel and his offering: but unto Cain and to his offering He had no respect. And Cain was very wroth, and his countenance fell. And the Lord said unto Cain, 'Why art thou wroth? And why has thy countenance fallen? If thou doest well, shalt thou not be accepted? And if thou doest not well, sin lieth at the door. And unto thee shall be his desire, and thou shalt rule over him.[7]*

---

[7] *Genesis 4:3-7 – www.biblegateway.com*

Tragically, Cain failed to take heed to God's warning and eventually became so enviously jealous of his brother that he killed him. Amazing the first murder in the history of man came as result of one brother's jealousy over God's acceptance of his brother's worship. Cain's worship could've been received too if came from pureness of his heart.

In essence, Adam and Cain embodied the difference between being created and being born. Creation is really the creative thought and omniscient foresight of God. Before Adam was created, he was a thought. God said in Genesis 1:26, *"Let us make man in Our image, after our likeness."*[8] On the other hand from Cain, the first born man, the *birthing process* is the process through which God has chosen to manifest this human idea. It's in this process that something happens – God's perfect idea becomes encompassed by flawed materials. David so eloquently explains this truth by stating, *"Behold, I was shapen in iniquity; and in sin did my mother conceive me."*[9]

The truth is the first battle ground of who we are begins in the womb. When we were conceived we inherited the same sinful nature as our father and mother just as Cain

---

[8] Genesis 1:26 – *www.biblegateway.com*
[9]*Psalm 51:5 KJV – www.biblegateway.com*

did from Adam. It's one of the basic fundamental truths that most of mankind refuses to accept – we were born sinners. However perplexing of a reality it is to grasp, God wrapped His perfect agenda (Purpose) with imperfect material (our flesh).

To make matters even more interesting, we've been divinely given the beautiful, but often times fatal, intrinsic ability of free will. God, the Creator, gave us the creative ability to choose to receive His original plan for our lives or to go on our own futile path of self will. How about that for a conundrum.

When we're born we essentially become captive to the sinful nature and often times the sinful culture we were born into. The moment we are conceived in the womb of our mother from impregnation of the seed of our father, we are inbreeded with a sinful nature that is automatically enmity with God himself. As result, we are by nature incapable of pleasing God though our own merits.

There are not many other people in the Bible whose birth exemplifies this more than Jacob, let's take look at the biblical account of his birth. The Bible states:

And when her days to be delivered were fulfilled, behold, there were twins in her womb. and the first came out red, all over

*like a hairy garment, and they called his
name Esau. And after that came his brother
out, and his hand took hold on Esau's heel;
and his name was called Jacob.*[10]

This man was supplanting from the very beginning. From the first time he saw the light of day, he was looking to usurp his brother, but yet within this fragmented beginning God's divine purpose was at work.

As you were reading this chapter you've probably seen bits and pieces of yourself within the lives of these biblical narratives and hopefully you're starting to get a clearer picture of who you are. Then there some of you who still have unanswered questions. Don't lose hope, this was your first step to discovering the real *you*. Stay with me my friend for in next chapter we're going to take a step further in this journey by venturing to the place where it all started, because the best way to understand who you've become is to study where you've been.

---

[10] *Genesis 25: 25,26 – www.biblegateway.com*

PART III
SAFE PLACE

Most of who we have been shaped and molded by where we were raised and by whom we were raised. My spiritual father, the late Bishop D.C. Thomas, once used the analogy that if he, being an African American, raised a child of Spanish descent from birth, that child would grow up not knowing one bit of Spanish (take my word for it he's telling the God honest truth). Now as simple as the analogy may be, it reveals to us a very profound truth. The language of where and who raised you has an in depth effect on how you communicate the world around you. I'm not just talking about verbal communication; I'm talking about your overall interaction whether it's in your perception of others or how you treat others, it all starts in the plant bed of the family.

Acclaimed author, Gary Chapman, wrote a book centered on marital relationships called, *The Five Love Languages*. In it he presents the idea that we are relationally wired into one of five love languages which frankly indicates how we give, receive, and see love. It is a great book and I highly recommend it for all married couples. Now, if you would indulge me for a moment I would take it a step further and say that every individual has a life language. A language that was taught to you from the time you were born that has shaped how you view life.

This has shaped how you dream. If you were raised in a home that speaks German, you wouldn't dream in English, would you?

Your environment is critical in how you envision yourself. Unfortunately, many of us have been raised in an environment of trauma. Most of this trauma goes untreated and eventually surfaces at times in our lives that are inopportune. Trauma, if untreated can eventually alter how one perceives reality around them. You call your enemies your friends, and your friends your enemies. The most damaging effect, however is that one will eventually find themselves, unknowingly, creating more trauma trying to escape trauma.

One of the elements of self-discovery I believe that is overlooked is the appreciation of the impact that community has on discovering oneself. The community that you are born in will shape the community within. For this reason, I can determine who you are by the people you surround yourself with. This perspective goes even further in regard to the family dynamic in which one is raised. How you were raised, good or bad, has shaped who you've become.

I believe that humans are embedded with the inclination to trust or distrust from the time that they were an infant. If a child is raised in an environment where there is neglect or a lack validation of one's intrinsic worth, that child will grow up looking for validation in other people; the first agency that lays the foundation or blueprint of one's view of self is the community one is birthed in.

In order for us to gain proper context of who Jacob was and how he came to be a patriarch of a nation, we have to first gain perspective of the family dynamic that has now developed. Genesis 25:27-28 reveals a very fascinating insight of the family culture that existed within Jacob's home. The Bible says:

> *And the boys (Jacob and Esau) grew: and*
> *Esau was a cunning hunter, a man of the*
> *field; and Jacob was a plain man, dwelling in*
> *tents. And Isaac loved Esau, because he did*
> *eat his venison: but Rebekah loved Jacob.*[11]

I want you to notice that the Bible took time to bring to our attention that Isaac *"loved Esau"* but Rebekah *"loved Jacob."* This sheds light on the brewing sibling rivalry that began, not with brothers themselves, but with unbalanced affections displayed by the parents. It isn't too farfetched to imagine that there was possibly a certain level of resentment built up between Jacob and his brother Esau

---

[11] *Genesis 25:27-28 – www.biblegateway.com*

while vying for the other parent's affection. Jacob no doubt grew to resent the level of relationship Esau had with their father, Isaac; Esau jealously noticing how Isaac took extra time teaching Esau how to hunt, showing him how to properly shoot an arrow.

I can imagine Isaac showing a level of frustration when Jacob didn't catch on as fast as Esau did. I can certainly picture Isaac saying these words to Jacob, *"Go back inside with your mother,"* or even more piercing, *"Why can't you be more like your brother?"* Maybe Jacob became a tent dweller because the tent became a *safe place*. All of us have *safe place* to run to when confronted with challenges or things that make life difficult. Our *safe place* is like Lionel's blanket from Peanuts, it's always close by so that we can easily grab it. When the fear of rejection comes we run back to the tent. When we struggle with acceptance we run back to the tent. When we struggle with identity we run back to the tent. We retreat back to our *safe place*.

Everyone's *safe place* can be different. It can be a toxic relationship, a job you settled for or a habit one can't kick. For some of us it can be something far detrimental like a toxic self-evaluation. Whenever triggers occur our minds immediately travel to, *"maybe I don't deserve it, maybe I'm not good enough or maybe I'm not worth loving."* Sometimes negative thinking can become a *safe place* when it's something you've become accustomed to.

Now to be fair, all *safe places* are created equal. Your family, your marriage, healthy relationships should all be a *safe place* that one should feel loved and accepted. However, may I suggest that for some of us it's our *safe places* that's keeping us from discovering who we really are? We stay where it's *safe*. We don't take risks unless it's *safe*. We struggle to forgive and reconcile with people because to forgive is to make one vulnerable and to be embittered and walled off is a *safe place*. We all have found ourselves at one time or another imprisoned in the confines of a tent that has become our *safe place*.

As we close this portion of our journey, allow me to challenge us with this notion: you can only discover the real you on the other side of *safe*. An unborn child is conceived in the womb, nourished through the umbilical cord and for 36 weeks the womb is all they know. The womb has become their *safe place*, but the unborn child doesn't become a child until they're thrusted out of their *safe place*. I believe that by the end of our journey we will be thrusted into who we were always purposed to be.

There's one thing, however that I must caution you on, and it is this: if we are going to be thrusted from our *safe places* we must be willing to come face to face with the very thing that coerces us to retreat there in the first place. We must be willing to address the very thing that shaped who we've become – trauma.

PART IV
WHEN TRAUMA DEFINES YOU

I recall an article I once read heralding the courage of a young rape victim who daringly chose to testify against her accused rapist. As I recollect, the prosecution did not necessarily need her testimony in order to gain the conviction because the physical evidence was sufficient in itself. It was the victim that insisted on taking the stand. When asked why she did it she simply replied that she refused let her attacker keep her power. Her courage revealed something that many of us have failed to realize; what you refuse to confront will inevitably have power over you.

Many of us have been paralyzed and restricted in our personal development because of a defining moment or period of time in our lives. Whenever emotional triggers arise, we mentally go retreat back to our *safe places* and cease from exploring *who* we've been created to be. In layman's terms, what we refuse to confront will eventually shape and mold some aspect of our character and personality. However, before we gain a proper understanding of what defines us, let us first understand the power of the word *definition*. When I looked up the word *definition*, Merriam-Webster gave several meanings of this particular word and here are just a few:

Definition –

1. *A statement of the meaning of a word or word, group or a sign or symbol*
2. *An act of determining*
3. *Sharp demarcation of outlines or limits*

Now, all of these aforementioned definitions are very impactful, but this definition I believe is the most relevant in the discussion of identity.

4. *A statement expressing the essential nature of something.*[12]

This crystalizes the power of *definition*. The definition one applies to a person or thing can be perceived as the expression of the very nature of the person or thing. If this definition is widely agreed upon and is universally accepted as being true, it then becomes an absolute truth. For example, one argues the nature of water. No matter who was the first human being to construct the first comprehensive definition of it, we all have unilaterally accepted water for being water.

A definition is a label that if you hear it long enough and consistently enough, you'll eventually become its meaning. It will be the name that you will inevitably respond to and take on its nature. Let's flash back if you

---

[12] [12] *Definition – www.merriamwebster.com*

will, to Jacob's birth, when Jacob exited from his mother's womb he was holding on to his brother Esau's, heel. As a result, he was named Jacob which in Hebrew means to supplant. And throughout Jacob's life whenever faced with difficulty or the opportunity to achieve an ambitious goal, he simply lived out the definition that was given to him. The only thing that defining moments do, is reveal the self-definition we have adhered to the whole time. Sometime storms don't make you, they reveal you.

Here in lies the ultimate questions for this part of our journey – who or what is responsible for our initial definition? Who or what has shaped the meaning of *me*? Who or what has definitively epitomizes the *who* I am at this juncture of my life. The answer that is true for most, if not all, is trauma. Whether it is unresolved childhood trauma, or it's from an abusive adult relationship, all of us are dealing with some level of PTSD incurred on us as a result of a traumatic event.

Trauma, if properly dealt with and harnessed, can produce greatness and bring one to a level of elevation into a higher consciousness of oneself. However, for many of us that is not the case. How we have addressed trauma has made us stuck. We have been so paralyzed by the fear of facing the trauma that it has inadvertently become our *safe place*. Our trauma has become our definition. We are drawn to this trauma like a moth to a flame, and meeting its same fate of being consumed by the traumatic cycle that ensnares us.

The harsh reality is that many of us have been labeled or defined in the mind of others and more importantly our own, by the trauma that birthed us. This was definitely the case for Jacob. Jacob had become defined by the simple act of holding on to his brother's foot while they exited their mother's womb. Now here's a fascinating perspective. What if Jacob was only trying to survive? Some trauma occurred as an inadvertent consequence to one's choice to survive.

Many people will try to define us by the drama and chaos we may have been born into or traumatic upbringing we were raised in without the understanding that we were just trying to survive. Some of the trauma that we have experienced is a byproduct of the need to survive; whether the original intent was for someone else's or our own. Some of us were put up for adoption because our biological mother was not ready to raise a child. Some of us were neglected by our parents because they were so consumed by their own need to emotionally and mentally survive the pressures that they themselves felt caving in.

Nevertheless, no matter what the intent may have been, and despite the contextual understanding that one can apply to the circumstances, the end result is the same – trauma. And if trauma is allowed to any portion of who we are, it will as a result pervert our view of ourselves and the world around us. How many of us have settled for less simply because trauma said that we were not good enough? How many have settled for the role trauma has dictated to us? How many of us have dated individuals that fit the profile of our attacker? How many of us have self-sabotaged relationships because they didn't fit in our traumatic cycle of dysfunction?

If we can identify with any of the aforementioned questions (which I believe most of us do) then trauma has defined some area of your life. And if we allow trauma to write the final epitaph on any area of our life we will fail to become *who* we were meant to be. We will prevent ourselves from seeing the truth in its unparalleled beauty. In order to discover the *who* that still exists within us, we first must remove the scar tissue that trauma has left behind and the only way to do it is to face it. We must be like that courageous girl who dared to face the one who raped her and as a result changed her definition from rape victim to rape survivor. It is not the trauma itself that makes us who we are, it is how we respond to trauma that make us who we are. Now that we have decided to face the trauma that tried to define us, we must now tackle the hard task of tearing down the *who* that trauma has created. I know it's been difficult but we are halfway through the journey of becoming *who* we really are.

PART V
RENOVATION

One of my favorite biblical narratives in the Bible is the account of God using the real-time illustration of the handy work of the potter to bring to light the nature of His relationship with the Jewish nation. Here is what it says according to Jeremiah 18:1-6:

> *¹The word which came to Jeremiah from the Lord, saying,*
>
> *² Arise, and go down to the potter's house, and there I will cause thee to hear my words.*
>
> *³ Then I went down to the potter's house, and, behold, he wrought a work on the wheels.*
>
> *⁴ And the vessel that he made of clay was marred in the hand of the potter: so he made it again another vessel, as seemed good to the potter to make it.*
>
> *⁵ Then the word of the Lord came to me, saying,*
>
> *⁶ O house of Israel, cannot I do with you as this potter? saith the Lord. Behold, as the clay is in the potter's hand, so are ye in mine hand, O house of Israel.*[13]

---

[13] *Jeremiah 18:1-6 – www.biblegateway.com*

What I find fascinating is that though the clay was *"marred,"* the potter didn't cast it away and bring in a whole new piece of clay. He simply worked through how marred the clay was and made it into what he desired it to be.

One of the misconceptions that come with facing one's trauma is the lie that what we have endured has diminished our intrinsic value. It is this deception I believe that doesn't allow many people to bounce back from tragic events in their life. *"If I was so valuable and my life had so much meaning, then why did this happen to me?"* This is the question that often times bombard our mind when coping with life. In reality what we find ourselves dealing with doesn't take away our value no more than the flaw within the clay diminished its value in the eyes of the potter.

What the potter simply did was renovate what was already there. Many of us may feel as if we have to create *new* material to become who we really are when in actuality, all we need is a renovation from within. Now, that's the primary focus of this part of our journey together; renovation begins within and not on the outside. One of the problematic approaches people sometimes have in regard to self-transformation is that we are quicker to change the outward appearance before we ever address the inward work necessary for change to be a reality. Plastic surgery and body enhancements only mask the dysfunctional image that we project on ourselves in our head. That new promotion or that new professional achievement will not fill that hollow void within. No matter how we try to dress the outside up, the renovation to discover one-self must begin within.

Please allow me to reaffirm this truth if we are embarking on this part of our journey that simply means that the fundamental framework of our existence still has value and is structurally sound enough to be salvaged and restored. If you are reading this portion of this book this includes YOU! No good contractor attempts to renovate any building that is not structurally worth the investment. However, though the framework of the house is good, we have to go through each room to deconstruct what was in order to reveal what can be. There are specific lies that trauma drove us to believe and accept as truth. These lies have built up walls that restricted our free movement into who we were originally purposed to become. Here are three general deceptive statements that we must demolish in order to properly renovate our thinking within our own minds.

1. *I am who I came from and the trauma I was born into.*

The old aged, *"the apple don't fall far the tree,"* has been used often times to connect the behavior of a particular child to that of a parent. First and far most, I believe that there's some truth to that; there some inherited personality traits that we all have received from our parents. Let's refer back to Jacob for a brief moment, Jacob desired his older brother Esau's birthright which was due to the first born by the laying on of hands by his father, Isaac. Jacob was not the only one who felt the birthright was rightfully his; his mother Rebecca shared the same sentiment. Rebecca in turn devised a plan to deceive Isaac into imparting it to Jacob instead of Esau. Here's the biblical account according to Genesis 27:5-17:

> [5] *Now Rebekah was listening as Isaac spoke to his son Esau. When Esau left for the open country to hunt game and bring it back,* [6] *Rebekah said to her son Jacob, "Look, I overheard your father say to your brother Esau,* [7] *'Bring me some game and prepare me some tasty food to eat, so that I may give you my blessing in the presence of the Lord before I die.'* [8] *Now, my son, listen carefully and do what I tell*

you: [9] Go out to the flock and bring me two choice young goats, so I can prepare some tasty food for your father, just the way he likes it. [10] Then take it to your father to eat, so that he may give you his blessing before he dies." [11] Jacob said to Rebekah his mother, "But my brother Esau is a hairy man while I have smooth skin. [12] What if my father touches me? I would appear to be tricking him and would bring down [13] His mother said to him, "My son, let the curse fall on me. Just do what I say; go and get them for me." [14] So he went and got them and brought them to his mother, and she prepared some tasty food, just the way his father liked it. [15] Then Rebekah took the best clothes of Esau her older son, which she had in the house, and put them on her younger son Jacob. [16] She also covered his hands and the smooth part of his neck with the goatskins. [17] Then she handed to her son Jacob the tasty food and the bread she had made.[14]

Let's take note how cunning Rebekah's plan was to deceptively attain the birthright on Jacob's behalf. She

---

[14] *Genesis 27:5-17 – www.biblegateway.com*

mapped out every detail to ensure that Jacob successfully received the blessing. This level of adeptness to trickery was shared with her older brother and Jacob's uncle, Laban. He tricked Jacob into marrying his oldest daughter, Leah, after he had already worked seven years to acquire the hand of his youngest daughter Rachel. Talk about no honor among thieves.

Jacob's father's side of the family wasn't that far better in regard to deception. Abraham, Jacob's grandfather, lied to the king of Egypt claiming that his wife, Sarah, was his sister going as far as allowing him to marry her. His father, Isaac was guilty of the same lie as his father before him. Pretty much it is abundantly clear that lying and deceiving was embedded in Jacob's genetic makeup. Many of our dysfunctional traits are associated with generation cycles. And these cycles, if not broken, can and most likely will be repeated in one generation after another.

The only way this cyclical behavior can be broken is when one makes the choice not to perpetuate previous failures of past generations. This is what Jabez realized when he made the decision not to be defined by the label and family trauma he inherited. Here is the Bible's account of Jabez according to 1 Chronicles 4:9,10:

⁹And Jabez was more honourable than his brethren: and his mother called his name Jabez, saying, Because I bare him with sorrow. ¹⁰And Jabez called on the God of Israel, saying, Oh that thou wouldest bless me indeed, and enlarge my coast, and that thine hand might be with me, and that thou wouldest keep me from evil, that it may not grieve me! And God granted him that which he requested.[15]

Jabez did not allow the name his mother gave him or the dysfunctionality he was born into dictate to him *who* he would become. We cannot allow our past to paralyze our future.

2. *I am not adequate enough for purpose.*

To be honest, second guessing yourself is par for the course. Sometimes self-doubt is a sign of self-awareness and serves as a counterbalance to becoming overconfident and arrogant. However, when self-doubt cripples us from purpose it can become suicide. There are many biblical and historical figures who when faced with adversity had to overcome the dissenting voices from

---

[15] *1 Chronicles 4:9,10 – www.biblegateway.com*

within. Abraham Lincoln had to overcome depression while trying to hold together an entire nation. Moses had to lead a people with a shepherd's staff and a stutter. The list can go on and on, but the one that stands in the forefront of my mind is a man by the name of Gideon. Gideon was a farmer in the Bible during the time in which the Jewish people were oppressed by the Midianites. From the very beginning a poor self-perception was a challenge. Judges 6:14-16 says:

> The Lord turned to him and said, "Go in the
> strength you have and save Israel out of
> Midian's hand. Am I not sending you?
> "Pardon me, my lord," Gideon replied, "but how
> can I save Israel? My clan is the weakest in
> Manasseh, and I am the least in my family."
> The Lord answered, "I will be with you, and you
> will strike down all the Midianites, leaving none
> alive.[16]

Gideon's low self-esteem was hindering his ability to know that despite his flaws he was made of the right stuff to fulfill purpose.

Do you not know that area in your life that is *"marred"* was permitted with purpose in mind? The

---

[16] *Judges 6:14-16 NIV – www.biblegateway.com*

Creator, who is the master sculptor, does not throw you away because you are marred. No, on the contrary our flaws often time is proof that we are adequate for the purpose we're created for. People who have survived childhood trauma become the most effective counselors for those have suffered from the same trauma. What if your flaw was a part of your purpose? What if the marred area of your life was a foreseen allowance the Potter factored in as a part of the process?

In music theory there is occasionally a note in the score called a mistake; this note isolated in by itself is not even in the key signature of the song, but when included with the surrounding notes it adds color and beauty to the song that would not exist without it. We cannot allow our inadequacies to block our view of this truth: we're tailor-made for our distinctive purpose – flaws and all. This leads us to our final misnomer that we need to demolish.

3. *I have to prove that I am worth loving*

It seems as if love or being loved is sometimes overlooked when discussing identity when in actuality it is the breeding ground in which it is formed and cultivated. To be honest the previous two deceptive statements that we have sledgehammered are a byproduct of the question surrounding love. Being loved produces the strength and conviction that I am loved beyond my past, therefore, my past cannot keep me from becoming. Being loved also allows me fearlessly and without shame to embrace my flaws knowing that they don't make me less or more loved.

Unconditional love is the essential basic existential need in all of us. We will look for it first from our parents, who ideally we expect to instinctively exemplify that for us when we involuntarily entered into this world. When we don't receive it we are left with a void that only love can fulfill. Some of us try to fill this by accomplishing things that would garner the adulation of people around us. Some of us become selfish, and as result we become cold in our dealings with love. And some of us struggle to the point that we find ourselves fighting to prove that we are worth loving.

Now, worth is determined by what someone is willing to give up for it. And worth and value is oftentimes subjective. What you may deem as valuable may differ from what I see as valuable. Often times what sets the mark for everyone else is what one person is willing to pay in an auction for a particular item. Let us see what the Creator from the biblical narrative was willing to give for the world. John 3:16 says, *"For God so loved the world that he gave his one and only Son, that whoever believes in him shall not perish but have eternal life."[17]*

That's a steep price tag don't you think? The Creator according to the Bible, deemed our collective value to be worth His only and best. Now, that worth and value mean that it was based upon something that we could offer or some act that we could perform? No, to the contrary we were powerless and quite frankly offensive to the Creator when He decided to pay that bill.

Romans 5:6-8 states:

You see, at just the right time, when we were still powerless, Christ died for the ungodly. Very rarely will anyone die for a righteous person, though for a good person someone might possibly dare to die. But God demonstrates his own love for us in this: While we were still sinners, Christ died for us.[18]

So does that mean that we are able to receive this based off of our performance? No, we come into the actualization of the benefits of this already available love through our faith to believe and His that must be received:

---

[17] *John 3:16 NIV – www.biblegateway.com*
[18] *Romans 5:6-8 – www.biblegateway.com*

Ephesians 2:8-9 says:

> *For it is by grace you have been saved,*
> *through faith—and this is not from*
> *yourselves, it is the gift of God— not by*
> *works, so that no one can boast.*[19]

Here in lies the crux for me when I observe all of the other major world religions, whether it's monotheist or pantheist, your reward or receiving their approval is performance based. That's one of the reasons why radical Islamic followers are able to convince young impoverished Islamic young men to give their lives under the presumption of a holy war. For them and their family it means they'll be automatically granted access into paradise bypassing the scales of the weighing of deeds on judgement day. This goes the same for religions that subscribe to the notion of reincarnation.

There is one religion; however, that begins the conversation with this truth: if based upon merit of performance none of us is good enough. On our best day we could do nothing that could earn the love or intrinsic approval of the Creator's love. You are intrinsically loved simply because you exist. Love is not earned; it is given.

---

[19] *Ephesians 2:8-9 – www.biblegateway.com*

Kobe Bryant once said in an interview that what unlocked his basketball genius is the affirmation he received from his father as young kid after a bad game. His father simply told him, *"win or lose your still my son."* It was the brief affirmation of identity that subsequently gave Kobe the confidence without fear of failure. Love in its purest form removes fear and 1 John 4:18 reminds us that, *"There is no fear in love; but perfect love casteth out fear: because fear hath torment. He that feareth is not made perfect in love."*[20] Don't live in fear but be released in the Creator's love. This next portion of journey will bring us closer to who we really are by unravelling the substratum of all existence: *the Source.*

---

[20] *1 John 4:18 – www.biblegateway.com*

PART VI
THE DECONSTRUCTION OF THE CREATOR

One of my favorite philosophers is a German philosopher by the name of Fredric Niche. Now for those who are familiar with his work will find this too surprising considering that he was a seminary student who became an atheist. As a matter of fact he was one the foremost philosophical thinkers who pushed the societal migration from a theist moral social construct to a more humanist framework. One of my favorite poems is Niche's "Parable of a Madman." Here are some powerful excerpts from that poem:

Have you not heard of that madman who lit a lantern in the bright morning hours, ran to the marketplace, and cried incessantly: "I seek God! I seek God!" -- As many of those who did not believe in God were standing around just then, he provoked much laughter. Has he got lost? asked one. Did he lose his way like a child? asked another. Or is he hiding? Is he afraid of us? Has he gone on a voyage? emigrated? -- Thus they yelled and laughed.

The madman jumped into their midst and pierced them with his eyes. "Whither is God?" he cried; "I will tell you. We have killed him -- you and I. All of us are his murderers. But how did we do this? How could we drink up the sea? Who gave us the sponge to wipe away the entire horizon? What were we doing when we unchained this earth from its sun? Whither is it moving now? Whither are we moving? Away from all suns? Are we not plunging continually? Backward, sideward, forward, in all directions? Is there still any up or down? Are we not straying, as through an infinite nothing? Do we not feel the breath of empty space? Has it not become colder? Is not night continually closing in on us? Do we not need to light lanterns in the morning? Do we hear nothing as yet of the noise of the gravediggers who are burying God? Do we smell nothing as yet of the divine decomposition? Gods, too, decompose. God is dead. God remains dead. And we have killed him.

"How shall we comfort ourselves, the murderers of all murderers? What was holiest and mightiest of all that the world has yet owned has bled to death under our knives: who will wipe this blood off us? What water is there for us to clean ourselves? What festivals of atonement, what sacred games shall we have to invent? Is not the greatness of this deed too great for us? Must we ourselves not become gods simply to appear worthy of it? There has never been a greater deed; and whoever is born after us -- for the sake of this deed he will belong to a higher history than all history hitherto."

It has been related further that on the same day the madman forced his way into several churches and there struck up his requiem aeternam deo. Led out and called to account, he is said always to have replied nothing but: "What after all are these churches now if they are not the tombs and sepulchers of God?"[21]

What makes this poem so riveting is that while it is claiming the *"death"* of God, within it exposes the logical existential struggle we encounter when we absolve ourselves from the belief in a transcendent Creator. The question of morality has become the major sticking point for many secular philosophers throughout time when they remove the belief in an absolute Lawgiver. Relativism is an argument that has contradicted itself purely of off common sense. If what I believe is morally right, is solely left to my discretion without being measured by a transcendent universal moral law adjudicated by a transcendent Lawgiver, then we have to now release every child murderer and can no longer convict rapists simply because they deemed their crime as the right thing to do in their own eyes.

If a proposed truth cannot be deconstructed and effectively rebuilt to its original proposed premise then it

---

[21] *Poem: Friedrich Nietzsche, The Parable of the Madman (1882); www.historyguide.org*

is no longer truth. Let's take the notion of this whole universe being constructed by chance and apply it to a simple example of a messy room. If your room is utter chaos, I would like for you to apply this logic by balling up as many clothes as you can, stand on top of your bed, and hurl them everywhere, and expect them by chance to be neatly folded and put away in the dresser. The only way that room is going to be clean is if you, a being whose existence and power transcends any object in the room, intelligently and with intention move and organize everything in that room.

In retrospect its ironically fitting that Niche titled the poem *The Parable of a Madman*; it is a maddening quest to disprove the existence of an intelligent and intentional Creator. I believe the Bible sums it up best in Psalm 14:1a when it says, *"The fool says in his heart, There is no God."*[22]

I believe that many people who ascribe themselves as atheist aren't really atheist but rather skeptics – people who often question the existence of a supreme Creator in light of circumstances they attribute to His possible non-existence. How can the Creator exist and sit idly by and allow this level of anarchy to transpire? And if this

---

[22] *Psalm 14:1a – www.biblegateway.com*

Creator exists and He is good than why does all this suffering and evil exist in this world that He created?

I really wish that I could give a profound answer to these questions and I wish that the answer would be able to appease the intellect of biblical and secular scholars. All I have is this simple of truth: the Creator's greatest gift to mankind is more often times than not creation's greatest detriment which is the gift to choose. Absence of freewill is the absence of love. Love is only love when both parties have the freedom to choose. If the Creator did not create us with autonomy of choice He would not have created us unto love but rather to manipulation and control. Unconditional love without granting the one you love to have the power of choice is not love, it is control.

Unfortunately, we are more prone to make choices without the Creator's input. When choices are made consequences are created. The results of our choices are often more far reaching than what the initial choice initially appeared to be. Take for example of what to the naked eye appears as a non-consequential vote in a state senate meeting to change district lines by 3 miles. It would appear on the surface that it should have no impact on the upcoming congressional race. However, the choice to approve this redistricting may turn the vote in favor of one party over the other. This choice creates an easier path to political office for someone who may not vote in the best interest of those who live in that district. What I just describe is gerrymandering, a political strategy used in politics to gain an unfair advantage in elections.[23] These choices have a major impact on policies and legislation that is passed that has a direct and indirect effect on the economic agendas that impact poverty.

I used that example to bring to light the power of choice and how if not used with wisdom, it can impact people's lives and cause suffering. Now in one way the existence of freewill simply affirms the existence of the Creator, if one would ascribe the Creator of the biblical narrative. Here's what Genesis 1:26 says on this matter:

Then God said, "Let us make mankind in our image, in our likeness, so that they may rule over the fish in the sea and the birds in the sky, over the livestock and all the wild animals, and over all the creatures that move along the ground.[24]

Notice that the Creator made us *"in His image"* and *"in His likeness."* We are no more than mere carbon copies

---

[23] *Gerrymandering – www.britannica.com*
[24] *Genesis 1:26 – www.britannica.com*

of the original Blueprint. That is why Jesus, the Creator in the flesh, came on earth; to show us the blueprint of who we were meant to be. To try to identify oneself without acknowledging the Creator is equivalent to an architect trying to design a blueprint without using math. He is Aristotle's *"Unmoved Mover"* who moves but yet can't be moved; who creates and yet cannot be created. He is the *"First Cause"* of existence.

I regretfully have to hand it to Niche as he may have been partially right in the final clause of *The Parable of the Madman* when he wrote, *"What after all are these churches now if they are not the tombs and sepulchers of God?"* One of the harsh realities that I have come to face is that the church has lost its overall impact in the United States. I believe that we are heading towards becoming a nation of skeptics and spiritual humanists.

We have become a generation that is searching for identity and purpose, and we are not being effective "blueprints" that can be read because we are still trying to discover ourselves. We struggle to grasp who we are simply because we have constructed are own convoluted understanding of who the Creator is based off of religion and not out of relationship. And although any healthy relationship has healthy boundaries, relationship doesn't imprison you. On the contrary, relationship liberates you, and will at times remind you of your value. It was the prodigal's son remembrance of his father that reminded him that he did not have to settle for the pig pin.

Relationship brings meaning. It brings freedom. It reveals who we are. Let us center our focus on this truth: the treasure *who* we are differing from, from what we have become can only be discovered through an encounter with the One who placed the treasure within us. This leads us to the last part of journey: *The Encounter.*

PART VII
THE ENCOUNTER

"God comforts us into relationship, but wrestles us into identity."

-Rasan Warren

As I was trying to figure out how segway into this final part of our journey, the above quote from my dear brother resonated with me and epitomized the crux of discovering and becoming who you were created to be. The Creator comforts you into trusting the truth that He cares. He is lovingly silent as you unravel the trauma that has shaped your life, lending a listening ear accompanied with a still small voice. He is peacefully strengthening you as you renovate the rooms of your heart and mind, steadily reminding you that you can do this. He patiently waits as you discover who He really is, carefully guiding you through the corridors of His love for you. When it comes to identity however, the Creator becomes hands on, because only loving pressure can forge that.

When the Creator first created man, He hand-crafted Adam from the dust of the earth. What is fascinating is the rest of creation was spoken into existence, but in regard to creating man He decided to get His hands dirty. And to awaken the awareness of who we were created to be He must apply pressure to our lives to bring us out of who we have become into who He created and purposed us to be. The only difference between a lump of coal and a five carat diamond is the pressure that the five carat diamond has survived.

The reason why I believe that identity requires this somewhat abrasive approach is simply because the question of identity was a part of the deceptive part of the fall of man into sin. When the serpent was able to prey on Eve's lack of self–awareness of who she already was, he was successful in getting her to be a pawn in the game of ensnaring all of mankind. We see this in Genesis 3:1-5:

> *¹Now the serpent was more crafty than any*
> *of the wild animals the Lord God had made.*
> *He said to the woman, "Did God really say,*
> *'You must not eat from any tree in the*
> *garden'?"*
> *² The woman said to the serpent, "We may*
> *eat fruit from the trees in the garden, ³ but*
> *God did say, 'You must not eat fruit from the*
> *tree that is in the middle of the garden, and*
> *you must not touch it, or you will die."*
> *⁴ "You will not certainly die," the serpent*
> *said to the woman. ⁵ For God knows that*
> *when you eat from it your eyes will be*

opened, and you will be like God, knowing good and evil.[25]

Only if Eve knew that according to Genesis 1:26 she was created in the Creator's image and likeness she wouldn't have been deceived into eating something to become who she already was. As a result many of our essential decisions are made either from the premise of discovering who we are or affirming who we believe we are becoming. From professionals making multi-million dollar deals to a single mother making sacrifices for her children, all of our decisions are made with the fundamental understanding of who we are or who we have to be.

The harsh reality is that the outer workings of our life don't give us a full glimpse of who we really are. When one's true identity is realized it produces a fulfillment of purpose and a laser-type focus and drive that brings inner-peace even in the midst of chaos. Success without an inner sense of purpose will not bring you peace.

Let us go back to Jacob, by the time we see him in Genesis chapter 32, he has two wives, concubines, children, wealth, cattle, and sheep. As Jacob is about to

---

[25] *Genesis 3:1-5 – www.biblegateway.com*

return to his homeland to meet his brother, it would appear as if he possessed all that was entailed with the birthright that he received from his father, Isaac. However, the birthright gave him the blessing, but it didn't give him identity. There was still an inner battle with how he was created to be and the name he was conditioned to answer to.

It's this inner struggle that we all have faced in this life; the struggle between the you that you have been pre-conditioned to be and the *eternity* that has been placed within you that only the Creator has the ability to unlock. All of us at one time have struggled with living under an alias that we know deep down inside doesn't capture the fullness of our potential. This rebirth will not be painless. The exiting of the birth canal from who you are into who you were created to be can mentally exhausting and emotionally draining, but it will be worth it. The only way to do this part the Creator has to first isolate you by you isolating yourself. Notice what Jacob does:

> [22]*That night Jacob got up and took his two wives, his two female servants and his eleven sons and crossed the ford of the Jabbok.* [23]*After he had sent them across the stream, he sent over all his*

possessions. [24]So Jacob was left alone, and a man wrestled with him till daybreak.[26]

Jacob is fearful at this point of the impending face to face meeting with his brother, Esau, that he hasn't seen since he deceptively received the birthright that their father Isaac originally intended to give his older brother. All of this was orchestrated by the Creator; sometimes He will use your fear of facing your past to confront you about your future. Encounters are never public, they are private. The Creator will use moments of isolation to address identity, simply because we must have an understanding of who we are by ourselves so that we don't easily conform to the identity of others.

Secondly, the Creator must subdue our will. Now, this aspect of the encounter is a painful one. While we were living under the false pretense of who we were pre-conditioned to be, we all developed our own agendas. All of us have set up in our minds where we want to be in our lives. Many of us when we began this journey had already decided what kind of career we wanted to pursue and the kind of person we wanted to marry or even if we wanted to get married at all. All of our plans and desires

---

[26] *Genesis 32:22-24 – www.biblegateway.com*

are altered or at least subjected to question the encounter with the Creator.

Do you recall the biblical narrative we referred to concerning Jeremiah's visit to the potter's house? The potter did not confer with the clay whether or not it was going to be a pitcher or a cup. That clay was submissive to the hands of the potter as they shaped and molded it according to the purpose of the potter. When the Creator created you, He created you with purpose so distinctive for us that only the created us can fulfill. The catch is the Creator never curtails purpose to fit our plans. He will always interrupt our plans to fit within purpose.

Now, in order to subdue our will to His, He will often times touch us in a sensitive place. This is what happened in Jacob's face to face encounter with the man in Genesis 32:25. The Bible says, *"When the man saw that he could not overpower him, he touched the socket of Jacob's hip so that his hip was wrenched as he wrestled with the man."*[27]

Now, for those who don't know any lower extremity injury is debilitating, but none more painful than a hip injury. I once suffered a hip flexor injury and it was extremely painful, so I can only imagine the pain of a

---

[27] *Genesis 32:25 – www.biblegateway.com*

dislocated hip in the midst of a wrestling match. This no doubt produced some balance and mobility issues for Jacob which in turn made him dependent on the One he was wrestling with. In the encounter the Creator will touch us in areas of are dependency to force us to trust His will more than our plans. His will, His design, His purpose when allowed to have full reign in our lives is far more fulfilling than our own plans could ever produce.

Now, before we get to the last thing the encounter will do, I want to encourage us to have the tenacity of Jacob, who despite the dislocated hip held on. The goal of the Creator wasn't to see if Jacob could win the fight, but if he could hold on through the fight. Do not leave at the halfway point. Many of us have been to this point in our lives before and when things have gotten tough, or we faced adversity we settled for going back to the deceptive comfortability of status quo, just to be miserable with regret three years later. Now is the time to see this all the way through. What we are enduring right now in becoming our created selves does not compare to what we have already survived. We cannot abandon the process until we become.

We have to hold on with intentionality. Let's look at the verbal exchange between Jacob and the man in Genesis

32:26. It reads, *"Then the man said, "Let me go, for it is daybreak." But Jacob replied, "I will not let you go unless you bless me."*[28]

Notice that Jacob recognized the moment. This was the moment when Jacob decided that he wasn't leaving this encounter empty handed. He was determined to leave with more than he came in with. We cannot afford to leave this moment without becoming something greater. Now, what is intriguing is that when Jacob asked for a blessing, the man asked for a name. The Bible says:

> [26] *Then the man said, "Let me go, for it is daybreak." But Jacob replied, "I will not let you go unless you bless me."* [27] *The man asked him, "What is your name?"*
>
> *"Jacob," he answered.*[29]

You see, Jacob was used to advancement consisting of being blessed, he never envisioned being transformed. Many of us are guilty of miscarrying transformative opportunities because it's unfamiliar to us. When something is meant to transform us it stretches us into the unfamiliar. It forces us to expand our perception of who

---

[28] *Genesis 32:26 – www.biblegateway.com*
[29] *Genesis 32:26, 27 – www.biblegateway.com*

we really are. Look at the profound dialogue between Jacob and the Man, and let us take a special look at the Man's final affirmation of Jacob:

26 Then the man said, "Let me go, for it is daybreak." But Jacob replied, "I will not let you go unless you bless me." 27 The man asked him, "What is your name?"

"Jacob," he answered. 28 And he said, Thy name shall be called no more Jacob, but Israel: for as a prince hast thou power with God and with men, and hast prevailed.30

Jacob asked for a blessing, but the Man gave him a new name. It was the identity that was attached to who he was in his mother Rebekah's womb before the trauma of his birth caused him to be identified as someone else. Who we are really created to be was always in us, just buried under the trauma and the self-doubts that often times led to bad decisions. The created me was buried underneath the dirt and the encounter when the Creator pulled me out.

What is so breath taking is Jacob's *created* identity, Israel, was far greater than he could have imagined. There is a nation that bears his name which means that there

---

[30] *Genesis 32:26-28 – www.biblegateway.com*

was a nation buried within him. The reason why becoming who the Creator created you to be is so crucial is because the success of other people's journey to "becoming" is attached to yours. It may be a child in your family. It may be a co-worker on your job. It may be an old acquaintance from your past who remembers you while you was living under your false identity. It may even be those who present themselves as your enemy. Someone else's becoming is co-dependent upon yours. The Creator's overarching purpose is so vast and interconnected that though it includes you, it's far greater than just you. The world is waiting for the arrival of the real *you*, but you must first come to the revelation that *"There is another me in me."*

About The Author

Being the second born son of two preachers, it became known very early that Sherman was called to follow the footsteps of his parents. At an early age Sherman had begun showing signs of being a gifted orator; reciting Martin Luther King's *"I Have A Dream"* speech for talent shows and school plays. Sherman displayed that he had the niche for public speaking.

However, what the exposure to the writings of Dr. King and other great orators did was develop Sherman's love for writing. He marveled at the ability to paint a picture in readers' minds with words. He always believed that words, spoken or written, have the ability to allow people to see themselves in places they have never been before.

Sherman Boone Jr. is an Associate Pastor at World Alive Center located in Trenton N.J. He currently resides there with his beautiful wife, Seanna, and their wonderful daughter, Nalah. Being an ordained minister preacher for nearly 20 years, his undying passion to reach people with the message of hope has driven him to undertake endeavors, like *Revolution in the Park*, in an effort to fulfill what he believes to be his life's calling.

Although Sherman loves spreading the gospel and the transformative message of change, his greatest joy is spending time with his wife, daughter, and family. He believes that the greatest tragedy is a person living without purpose.

Made in the USA
Middletown, DE
16 March 2023

26884014R00046